Learning to Be Me

Learning to Be Me

Original Poems by
Daniel Ali

Illustrated by
Isabella Ali

A Gatekeeper Book

Learning to be me
Copyright © 2020 by Daniel Ali

ISBN 9798649170970
Cover design by Laura
Cover image courtesy of Placeit

For my children
Halimah, Sharrieff, Isabella, Kavi and Ma'ali.

Table of Contents

Introduction

At a very young age, I remember feeling that there was something I wanted to say. I felt it inside as strongly as the beat of my heart or the breath in my lungs. And even though I wasn't sure what it was that I wanted to say, I knew that writing was the way to do it. I've always loved writing and I learned early on that it was a comfortable way for me to express thoughts and feelings that I couldn't otherwise.

When I was eleven years old, I began keeping a daily journal. It kept me busy and satisfied my need for self-expression, even though I never shared what I wrote. All that changed when I heard my first Beatles record at the age of thirteen. Now the journal entries were not just endless rambling of my daily thoughts and ideas, they were poems and eventually songs as I was quickly learning to play the guitar, a talent I've developed over the years and continue to enjoy to this very day.

When I was in the ninth grade I took a Poetry and Mythology class at my high school in Atlanta Georgia. My teacher, Mrs. Lowe saw potential in my writing and encouraged me to continue and to share what I wrote with others. I thank her for that. Her encouragement gave me the confidence to push myself to grow my ability.

The poems in this book are a special selection spanning many years, some of them written as far back as the early eighties. They are an honest, unfiltered reflection of my journey on the way to learning to be me, a journey that has, in many ways, only just begun. I hope you enjoy this little book of poems, and if perhaps you find something of value to you in your own journey, well that's alright too.

Be a Butterfly

Did you stop to think when you was changing

That you just might leave someone hanging?

Did you stop to notice while your world was
turning around, that you was breaking the ground
—that you was tearing it down?

I know we all want to be free

And I'm not you and you're not me

But did you notice while your head was turning
around, that you was knocking it down —that you
was letting me down?

Did you know you was a Butterfly?

But you can blow it if you don't know why.

Or did you really think by racing out of your shell,
you'd have a story to tell —that you would make it
so well?

I know more than you might know, but that don't
mean I'm always right though.

But what I know is that you're turning round too
fast to see the broken glass and babe you might
not last

she said

She said, "you have beautiful brown eyes –a shade
different than most"
I was embarrassed –ashamed that I smiled inside
Could this be, the look in her eyes -reflecting me?
She's so beautiful and sees me as the object of
pretty?
Na, I've been here before –three times been on the
floor.
I make this too easy.
Detached heart, bleeding –no ointment to sooth me.
"What happened to you?" she asked –a pained
expression on her face.
"Is it really so hard for you to share your space?"
She touched my heart –cold down to the bone.
And there's been so many dark moons alone.
I wanna open up –let it free, but damn, those old
habits, they don't die easily
That voice keeps talking
You can't, you don't, you won't, and I dance, that
music –like a trance

Every adverse off-beat.
I can't compete, no cover from the heat.
I know she'll find me, remind me that all I did was
wrong.
Same old song in the key of pain, rejection and
blame.
But I'm not the same –sometimes people do change!
You never thought I'd get tired of fighting the cold,
Never dreamt I'd crawl out of that hole.
But I did, and now I'm free!
But I still can't believe it's me.
And you don't see. Not like her.
Her eyes light up for me.
Her arms reach out to comfort me
Her voice speaks soft and low to inspire me…
And FINALLY -I'm learning how to be me.

let the cage door swing

Every knock is a boost -or is it every
boost is a knock? Can't get the
knack
It seems every step forward gets
pushed three steps back.
I can't tell -is it me?
 Maybe I'm just not who you

suppose me
to be
Can't tell
you how
alone I feel
no matter
the crowds
that surround
me.
Empty. Can't
somebody see?
Help me if you can -I'm feeling
down
These tears blear my eyes like
Smokey's clown

All these emotions got me feeling
old
Like she said -you can't let go of
what you hold.
But I don't wanna do this no-more
I just wanna get away now
Leave it all behind -start again
somehow
I know why the caged bird don't
sing
Gotta let her go and let the cage
door swing

Maria and Tony

"So, tell me what we're gonna do now" she said
as they pushed the barriers, crossing the
treacherous waters of love onto the shores of
obsession.
A one-way trip with no stops, no recession, just
faith in one another and that magnetic attraction,
act and reaction, blind with a purpose, lost from
the surface.
Shy but not deferred, afraid but not deterred.
Crying out in the woods, lonely for the touch of
the other, close like God to mother, in synch like
planet and moon, dependent like fetus in the
womb.
360 degrees, a circle, not a square, out of line
and the love rotates in time. Spinning out of
control married in the soul, buried in a hole but
resurrected by fire through the cold
Is it really that old –its new again with you? I
see what others do not see, the wind blows life
through the tree, and the tree gives it back to me.
And again, it is you Maria always and forever.

It's not enough to have forever, connected like
matter and space, the gentle glow upon your
face. Am I deep enough, or shall I go deeper? As
much as it takes to reach her, she feels me in
tides, I fill her inside.
And together there is no end, no beginning just
forever and the day that follows, the night that
swallows, the hope that wallows and the truth
that hollows.
It is an eternity of love that covers the heart like
a glove from the coldness of this world.
You are my cover from the rain that pours and I
am yours.

in the shadow of my loneliness

I never knew that I needed someone, 'til I realized that I lost
your lovin'
I never knew that my heart would simply break and fall
apart.
I never knew that I'd ever miss you, never thought that I'd
wish I'd kissed you.
Now through the pain I've finally learned how to make a
start.

I never knew what it was to be
youthful, never knew what it
meant to be truthful.
Cause I was too busy doin'
what I had to do to be a man.
In the shadow of loneliness I sit
alone and I reminisce but, I
have learned that there is more
to love than just holding hands.
Sometimes in the middle of the
night I wake up to the cold
moonlight.

And feel the force that is pulling me against the reality that's
holding me down.
I walk out in the dark and the stillness, so weighted down I
can touch my illness
And fade to black as I sink beneath the world that is goin'
round.

I never knew that I needed someone 'til I realized that I lost
your lovin'
I never knew that my heart would simply break and fall
apart.
I've been living in a travesty, can't you see what it's done to
me?
In the shadow of my loneliness I've finally learned how to
make a start…how to make a start.
I made a start…I made a start…I made a start.

Superhero

Lightning reflected through me
I can't believe it's from me –I've
never been so unafraid.
You flash across my sky and leave
me wondering why...I'm saved
You take me
deeper and you
show me new
meaning so true
I finally learned
how to be me
You have released
me from the dark
inside of me
And now I'm free.
I'm free from the dark inside of me
I was lost when you came along
You put the prose back in my song
You put the love back in my heart
Showed I could make a start, if I
wanted to

I knew it was true, and so I
followed you
You helped me see what it is and
not what I want it to be
And not to let the negativity blind
me
You gave me strength to let love
show
And look inside –so now I can let it
go
You are the best that's in me
All the rest is empty –I've never
been so all aware
You have released me from the
dark inside of me
And I'm free
I am free, I'm free because you're
my Superhero
I am free…free…free because
you're my Superhero

IM FINE.

From My Experience

From my experience I've learned
Fool plays with fire –gets burned
U can't discover what's known
We all reap from what we've sewn
From my experience I've found
A negative mind state will bring you down
Some people they just never get free
One is too many for me

Everybody's so hooked on "I" feel
But what we don't know is that shit ain't even real
Nobody loves anymore –beloved tell me
What are we waiting for?

From my experience I've earned, sorrow and joy
in turn
I've watched the faces of time and –I've loved
them all in my mind.
From my experience I've gained
Faith in what some see as strange
I've seen where I've never been
But today it's all about learning the meaning
within

From my experience I've grown
I'm thinking now on my own
I thought I was being so strong but
I realize now that I was wrong

From my experience I've come
to learn to need someone
I've watched all the faces in my time
 —I've loved them all in my mind
From my experience I can say that LOVE is the
only way
It's not about what or how much we obtain, in
this life it's about what's in your brain and what's
in your heart that sets us apart
Because LOVE has become a spark lost in the
dark
But there's no need to fear me now —I've learned
the secret, LOVE is the answer —can you hear me
now?

Little Dove

How does it feel to be one of the beautiful people now that you're alive?

And would you believe in a love at first sight –tell me could you believe if you tried.

You are the best of all that I could ever have hoped I could ever become.

And now that I see your sweet beautiful innocence, I can't believe I'm the one.

You have exceeded my greatest imagination –you have redeemed my wounded soul.

A glimpse of the future riding wings of the Little Dove – watching the new world unfold –I'm just watching the new world unfold.

I was alone in this cold bitter world –needing a reason to smile.

You came along –a gift from the heavens a beautiful, beautiful child

So tell me today can you see what you mean to me –can you realize who you are?

You are the light in my darkest of loneliness –you are my
bright morning star.
My Little Dove you are bigger than earth –you are deeper
than eons of time.
You are the rain that cools, you are the sun that warms –you
are the thought in my mind.
Thank you for all the love you have invited me –thank you
for changing my world.
I'll never be alone, not with my Little Dove – beautiful,
beautiful girl
My little beautiful girl.

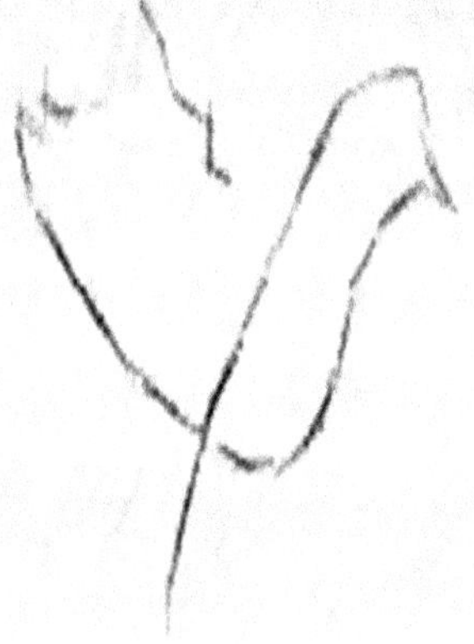

Ain't That a Sign

you wave your hand and from miles away
you change my day
you wink your eye and suddenly i die
then u breathe into
me and i rise -the
phoenix flies
—the pendulum
swings
and angels sing
your name and mine
ain't that a sign?
can't it be?
then why do u hurt
me
when u know i
would die 4 u
aint no wrong in me
and u
just us 2 and that
thing we do

i told u –ur the blood in my veins
my heart beats YOUR name
in a rhythm that's all u
and you're right –u do know me -but i know u 2
wat u r 2 me i should
i'm you're bad habit and you're mine
but damn –don't it feel good?

Beautiful Boy

I remember crying…thought I was dying.
It seemed the world had closed and left me
standing alone.
In your eyes I see through to the next
beginning.
Now I know I can change this heart of cold
stone.

When I hold your hand
I'm a happy man.
When I see your smile I
know there has to be a God.
There's so much inside of me I want to
share with you.
There's so much to learn in life and this
world can be so hard.
You can count on me…I'll protect your joy.
I will be there when you fall…you are my
beautiful boy.

When you go to sleep at night I will be your
safety light.
I will chase your fear away when ghosts and
monsters come to prowl.
You can hang your head on me when you
get weary.
When you're lost and can't find your way I
will surely show you how.

Hold your little hand in mine; I'll guide you
through the time.
I will shield you from the storm, I will never
steer you wrong.

Take your time you'll get things done.
You gotta walk before you run.
I send my love to you in this; my heart is in
this song.
You can count on me…I'll protect your joy.
I will be there when you call…you are my
beautiful boy.
Bet your life on me…my beautiful boy.

Albirda

I can see her eyes
as they shine –in
the deep of the
night
Piercing through
the realm of the
darkness –like a
beam of light
Soft sounds in the midnight hour –
sweet scent of her love
I've been inhaled by an angel –sent
from above

Albirda, can't you see, girl what you're
doing to me?

I can feel your breath get heavy –I
can taste your lips
I wanna feel your every emotion with
my fingertips
Deep waves from your roaring ocean,
covers me to my hair
I reach out from the depths of the
darkness but you're not there

Albirda, can't you see, girl what you're
doing to me?

I pretend when you flash your smile –
it doesn't matter at all
But every time that I walk away alone
–I feel two foot small
I wish I could just climb inside you –I
wish I could let it show
Oh God I'm in love with an Angel and
she don't know

Albirda, can't you see, girl what you're
doing to me?

A First Kiss

Another first kiss but more than this
And another once more
Ten thousand lost washed up on the
shore
The taste of Her mouth, the smell of
Her hair
Her skin -concupiscent musk, fills the air
Traveling in my mind through the barrier
that is time
i am free, and through the narrows my
eyes can see
A holographic image···She

Protected by time -a vision of a past
the future unborn
Or nothing at all
The beat of Her heart as She lay close
calls out to me
i am true but unsteady
Across the darkness we integrate, and
our rhythm orchestrates
Symphonic sensuality lingering until i am
overcome
The heavens empty as angels shower us
with tears
The gift of the First flesh - fresh and
unsoiled
A taste of Her temptation - sweet,
succulent
i am not un-nerved

Our compulsion, harmonic - free, and
unrehearsed
Even now the scent of Her is on me
She takes me with Her and leaves a
memory -i cannot escape
My prose flows from me like water into
the sea
It is easy because She inspires me
i ach for Her touch - i pain for Her
passion
And within Her i am proclaimed
Her form beguiles me - Her movements
exorcise
An Image surreal like diamonds between
Her thighs
And again, we climb to the cold side of
the sun
The planets run and the oceans turn
The flame consumes but does not burn

Gladys

Winter came much too soon
And plucked a flower, still in bloom
So, it's gone now but still, the light
shines
Through the memories of a lifetime
I remember Bergen Avenue
Walking home from school,
holding hands with you.
All the faces, how they
smiled at you
And the kind words - you
were smiling too.
Now my memories are my
only friend
Now my heart breaks, time and time
again!
Oh, Gladys, I miss you
I miss you

Now I'm older and I can see you
much more clearly than I used to.
I hear your wise words when I close my
eyes
I see your beauty in every loving
smile.
I remember breaking down in tears
how you held me and washed away my
fears
You were so sure that you would ease
the pain
And with your gentle touch made me whole
again
Oh, Gladys, I miss you

And in the Morning, We Made Love

I had dream —you called my name

I couldn't see you —but I came

And when I found

you —you turned to

stone

There I was alone

I climbed a mountain

—to kiss the sky

And if I reached it —

you are why

And we laughed

And cried

And held each other

tight

And in the morning,

we made LOVE!

LOVE, LOVE, LOVE, LOVE, LOVE

I had a feeling something wasn't right

I woke my lover late last night

I said my darling —I'm losing faith

I'm tired of running the race

She held me close and helped me to slow down

She told me "just let go and be found"

And she smiled

And sighed

And showed me deep inside

And in the morning, we made LOVE

LOVE, LOVE, LOVE, LOVE, LOVE

Affection

And if I ask you now...And if you tell me how...

Would it be the same?

Would it be the same?

And if I held your hand...What if I made a plan?

Would it spark the flame?

Would it feed the flame?

And if I asked you now...

All I want is you to be affectionate with me

And if I told you YES...What if I find the best?

Would it make a change?

Would it make a change?

And if I take it low...What if I play it slow?

Could it ease the pain?

What if I take the blame?

And if I tell you now...

All I want is you to be affectionate with me

All I want is you to be affectionate with me

All I want is you to be affectionate with me

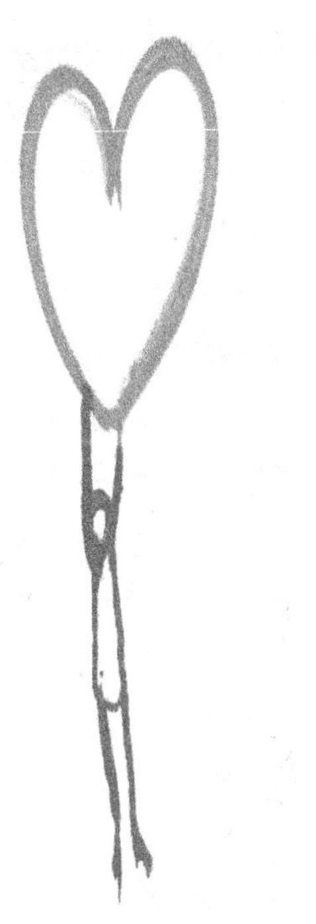

Never Love No More

How many more
tears can I cry?
How many ways
can I try?
Guess I'll never
close the gap
Never stop you
looking back
Always be, just
never quite right,
Like waves against
the beach
You retreat -always just out of reach
But my heart still beats for you
Slow even though I know -you really don't care
But I'm always there
Stuck between what was and what is -I am
positive
I swear, or at least I think I'm sure,
I'll never love no more
Not another like this again
Why, when I can't win?
Can't go another round
Too many times I've been put down

Getting punchy now -drunk from the pain
The loss of blood in vain
And my name is a curse on your lips
My tears drip like blood through your fingertips
And I am liquid.

Not Much More to Say

This is the worst part for me.
Is it me being strong or am I really a fool?
You could've heard my heart drop right through the line.
If you only listened JUST ONE TIME.
You do what you do to protect you.
I can't really say what you should do.
You say I'm jealous, maybe it's true.
But it aint for nothing, it's what you do.
I saw what you did with the last and before that too
Tried to believe it was more about me than you.
But I see your eyes roam -the distractions you hone
Careful you don't end up alone
You say that's fine -but I can read between the lines
I see how you try to hide
You only care how it looks from the outside
So here we are on our last breath
A shoebox full of nothing left
I admit it makes me cry

Always sad to see something beautiful die
Suicide, that's going out the worst way
Forgotten like trash on garbage day
Not much more to say
Throat thick with that sour regurgitated taste
Like that song, can't feel my face
Damn what a waste.

I miss YOU

*I miss you like flower misses Sun in the death of winter
-when the cold waters run*

*Like desert sands longing for days of old when waters
sprang in gardens wherein rivers flowed*

*I miss you like matter
before time spinning in
the deep of the mind of
HIM who created intent
-but had yet to evolve
to record his movement*

*Like the moon calling
out to the Earth*

*Like a lost lover on a
distant perch*

*Seeing but never to
touch*

*Forgotten but
remembering so much*

I miss you like the blood of life that flowed from Christ

*Like the heart of twin intertwined within from one yoke
separated but not broke*

*I miss you like blind eyes that once had sight and could
penetrate the light in spite of fears-but now behind
darkened glasses the light disappears*

I miss you from across the universe and back again

Between the raindrops and inside the wind

*I miss you from within the first seed in the root of the
old Oak tree*

But more than this, I miss you with me.

Miserably

I look across the raging waters and through the
scorched trees

Across the burning sands, the fertile lands ravaged
by locusts, grasshoppers and bees

And still I see you...

The crown jewel in my
heart, the Queen, like
Crystal speckled
Diamond - Ice Blue

And if after all this time
and all that we've been
through

If you still don't know that's who and what YOU
are to me

Then I have failed...miserably.

Breezin'

I was koolin' in Chiltown wit Mac
Daddy, Crusin' down by Newport in
his jacked up Caddy.
Wit' da windows down, wind blowin'
in a cross breeze
I felt at peace cause the scene put
my mind at ease.
I started thinkin' as we rolled by the
Pier, Manhattan looks so damn good
from here.
Bu then, wait a minute what a lovely
Face she was standin' all alone just
starin' into space.
Yo Mac Daddy stop the car I got a
habit.
A sweet tooth and she's so sweet, I
gotta have it.
So I stepped to her told her I was
Chil' Akey, she said yeah Chil...you
look good to me.

Told me her name was Krystal but I
could call her Kris, then she gave
me her number and gave me a kiss.
The way she looked the way she
moved was so pleasin' she left me
in a daze...I was breezin'.

 The next day I called her up cause
yo I missed her
My head was filled wit' images of
how I kissed her.
Her voice so sweet when she
answered the phone
said she was really glad I called plus
she was all alone.
When I got there she had incense
wine and candles
She made me wonder was she more
than I could handle.
I knew that love had finally caught
Me when she held me in arms and said
these words to me.
("You show me how deep love can be")

We made a move to the back on the
smooth tip
She made a move with her love that
made my mind trip.
Her skin was soft and brown her
eyes was clear and bright
She wrapped me in her lovin' all
through the night.
And in the morning when we finally
did awake, we both agreed together
that a family we would make.
And so I put an end to all the
endless skeezin'
I'm caught up in a daze and just
breezin.

The Ballad of Victoria Blackwell

So much un-
said —so much
passed over
my head
I never stopped to look —too much we didn't say
But today —I wonder what cover she's under
What name —what face she wears for the game
The one we used to play —that I never gave away
But it was in every word she couldn't say
And I couldn't see where my reflection blinded
me
Couldn't hear the rain in the cloud —the wind in
her hair was too loud
But he told me —he said she said it was true
But I can't take that shit from you
So I turned away even though I wanted to stay
Wanted to hear and know more
Hoped she'd leave the key under the mat by the
back door
It's funny how I walked in two directions at the
same time

Solid in my heart and confused in my mind
Just wasn't enough time, or it was actually to soon
Long before I began to bloom
By then she was gone —and I didn't even write a
song
But here I am —thinking about what she didn't say
What I couldn't hear but every day she blew kisses
my way
And I treated them like communion on Sunday
Drunk off the idea, the image —the thought
Like empty bags full of nothing she bought
Does that make sense?
Somehow it does —but it ain't what you think
It's not what I didn't hear —or what I never saw
It's so much more than she trusted me to know
And I stood outside her front door but didn't see
Victoria no more
And the stained glass she washed with her tears
are left behind in years of broken panes —shards of
forgotten things that remain
Things too weak to speak but weep instead
The wounded things not dead —bleeding for what
she never said
The falling hearts that never fell —forever sing the
Ballad of Victoria Blackwell.

Haven't I, Haven't You

Haven't I been wrong before?
Haven't you been right?
Haven't we had a world of love?
Why would we choose to fight?

Did I know that I didn't really know?
Did I ever try to hear?
Did it mean that you didn't really know
Just because it wasn't clear?

Can we learn to forgive if not forget?
Can we ever go that far?
Can we learn to accept and not expect?
Can we just be who we are?
Now I've learned to make my mistakes
Now I've got to find my own fate

Who was I when I said those things I said?
Did I speak right from my heart?
Where did I go when it came time to grow
up?

How could you take me from the start?

Haven't I been lost before?
Haven't you been sure?
Haven't I given less of my love?
Haven't you given more?

Now that my eyes can I see
And my heart can feel
I know you'll always be with me
And I know YOUR love is real.
Now I've learned to make my mistakes
Now I've got to find my own fate

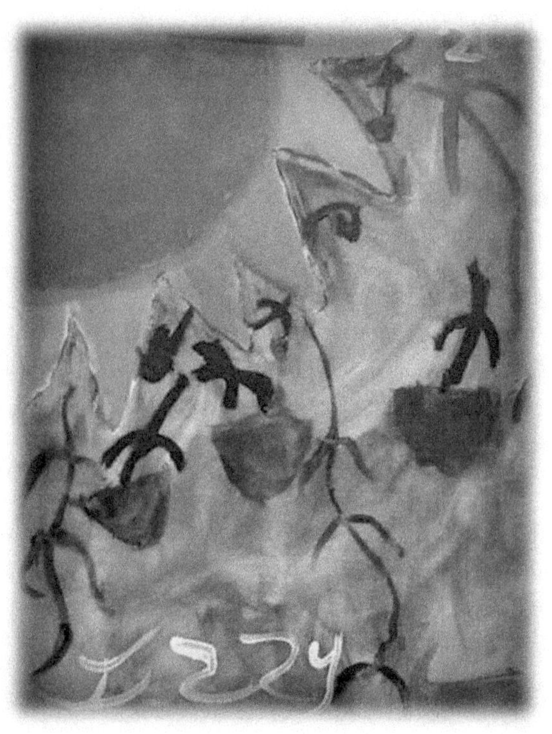

In the Isle of Patmos

As I stood there alone in the dark,
a light burned through my soul into my
heart.
About the light I heard a voice resounding
in the vast
The voice said to me, I am first and I am
last.
Don't turn away, write down what you
hear.
Don't cry for what you see and don't have
any fear.
The day is short, nightfall cometh soon
Fire from the depth of the sea, blood from
the moon.

And there was war in the heaven above
The war was claimed by the evil, lack of
LOVE
And from the throne he was cast down into
the sand
And from above him, I saw the hand of a
man
I am come
I am come
I am come

All We Ever Needed

All we ever needed was you and me
you
I swear its true, it's always been you
No matter how many came and
went
They were only time spent
Ever since that day at school, I
picked you out the crowd
I'd never seen a face so sweet, my
heart never beat so loud
I couldn't even think, couldn't hear
my thoughts
Remember standing on your mother's
porch?
I was so shy
When we kissed I thought I'd die
Loving, touching, squeezing

Every day, didn't need a reason
it was the season
For love, and love you I did and
I do, I will...forever and after that
too
All day it's you all night too,
everything I do,
I think, I wish, I want, I feel, I
am...it's still you.
If I never saw you again, got to
taste your kiss
It's not all I would miss
It's in your eyes and the way u smile
You are the blood in my veins, the
thoughts in my brain
And what remains is still you...
What can I do?
I'm lost inside you and you fill me
with you

Everything I think, everything I do
And it's still you
Now I'm deeper than I'd ever cared
Can't break free and I'm so scared.

The Burn Out

There's a girl in New York City, a thief who
stole my heart.
But she's gone away now and I'm alone, torn
apart.
I don't really care that she's never coming back.
Cause her kiss is lethal and her love's a heart
attack.

There's a boy I knew in school, he was a friend
of mine.
But he slipped along the way and now he's
fallen far behind.
He can't even see, though his eyes are wide as
the sky.
And he says he's finished here and now he just
wants to die.
All the pain feeds the flame of the burn out

Sometimes I sit alone and listen to the rain.
With every drop that touches earth, I fell a
thousand bursts of pain.
It's not all my fault and I still know the score.
Cause everybody pays and nobody gets what
they paid for.
All the pain feeds the flame of the burn out

There's a girl in New York City, she'll bow and
kiss your feet
She'll make you think that the world is yours
and give you kisses honey sweet.
But she just wants to hurt you, she loves the
taste of blood.
And yours is sweeter to her tongue cause your
smells of the stench of love.
All the pain, the pain. the burn out.

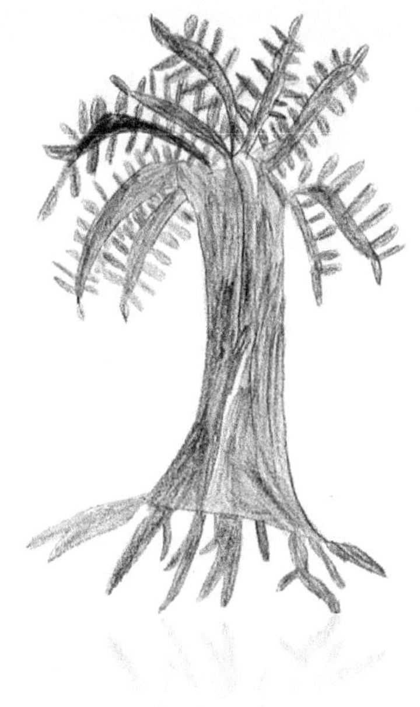

a common love action

Have you ever seen a man thrust
himself on a cold razor's edge?
I have.
Have you seen the soft gentle hand
that holds the blade?
Seen the eyes of heaven, that the
gates of hell betrayed?
Can u stand before them without
trembling?
Peering into your soul, your heart
weighed in the balance
Does it tip the scale against the
feather?
Does it take you past forever?
How can you know if you've never
tried?
How can you laugh if you've never
cried?
You can run but u can never hide

Mercedes Mishay

What a beautiful day
I never knew it could be this way
But there's something in her eyes
And I love the way she smiles

When she says hello to me
It makes me so happy
Just to know that she can see
All the love inside of me

I love the way her eyes shine
And the way she says she's mine
And even when we're apart
She's always in my heart
Mercedes Mishay
Mercedes Mishay

She makes me tremble from her stare
And the smell of her hair
I wanna love her all the time
And tell the world she's mine
Mercedes Mishay
Mercedes Mishay

What a beautiful day
I never thought I could feel this way
But there's something in her kiss
And my heart just can't resist
Mercedes Mishay
Mercedes Mishay

The Sound I Long to Hear

Wake up in the morning sun I see your
eyes.
Bathing in your morning dew, I feel my rise
Laughing in the moonlit sky, I taste your
kiss.
Yours is the sweetest love I know I'll never
miss

I love the way you gently sigh when I hold
you in my arms.
I love the way I love it when I'm wrapped
up in your charms.
I wish I could just climb inside you and fill
you 'til your passions yell.
Then maybe I could love you from inside
as well.

I stand in the cold and freeze in the rain
but you're not near.
I wait in the snow and wait for the sound I
long to hear.

Here I am and there you go and love's not on
your mind.
I'm trapped inside imagination lost in space
and time.
Can't you feel the pain I feel, can't you hear my
heart cry out?
I only wanna love you but you still seem to
doubt.

You're deep, deep inside my mind, you're
every breath take.
In visions of ecstasy sublime, you're all the love
I make.
Can't you see my heart's wide open, I give it to
you free?
The only thing I ask in return is you give your
love to me.

I stand in the rain and freeze in the cold but
you disappear.
I wait in the freeze in the snow and wait for
the sound I long to hear.

Afternoon Café
(Passion's Reverie)

Love, Love, Love
Love, Love, Love
Love, Love, Love
Love, Love, Love
Across a crowded room in an Afternoon Café he
noticed her
She sat so poised just like a beautiful flower
She was more beautiful than any woman he'd
ever seen
And even though she hadn't looked at him
directly,
He could the beauty emanating through her in
her eyes
Her movements excited him
Watching the extraordinary manner in which
she accomplished ordinary things left him lost
in a frenzy of daydreams
His mind could only imagine the sound of her
voice and the smell of her hair

The congestion in the room never seemed to
distract him from her
Not even for a moment
Who was she?
Where did she come from?
And why...why was she so beautiful?
In the middle of a room filled with people –
crowded making noise
The two of them were the only ones there
He thought to himself, maybe I should go and
speak to her.
Yes, I'll go over to her table and introduce
myself
So he got up and he walked across that room
filled with people making noise
And confronted the only other person in the
room
Smiling shyly he said...hello.
Love, Love, Love
Love, Love, Love
Love, Love, Love
Love, Love, Love

I Can't Do That

I can be your friend and tell you all that you
need to know.
I can hold your hand when times get rough
and not let go.
I can walk you home when you're alone and
you don't wanna be.
I can stay up late and play mind games or
watch TV.
But if you're looking for a love to last
through life, if you're looking for the dream
of man and wife.
If you're looking for a love...
I can't do that.

When you need a shoulder to cry on you
know what to do.
When your prize possessions bring you
down I'm here for you.

If you find you can't get satisfaction playing
that game.
If you find you've lost what you thought
was true just call my name.
But if you're wanting for a lover to fill your
heart, if you're wanting for another to make
a start.
If you're wanting for a love...
I can't do that.

I can be your friend and confident when
your head hangs low.
I can comfort you till you get strong then let
you go.
I can bring your water when you're sick and
need a drink.
I can change your mind when you're
confused and don't know what to think.
But if you're needing for the love of your
life,
If you're looking for the dream of man and
wife, if you're needing for a love...
I can't do that.

Slips Through My Hands

I can't believe what you, you do to me
I can't conceive of it – it can't be
I don't believe how you, you make me feel
I don't concede to it – it's not real
I walk away from it, it walks me back
I turn away from it, it turns me back
My eyes are open and I feel like a fool
I see it coming but I just play it cool
I wanna run away and hide in the sand
But when I touch the earth it slips through my
hands
I'm asking you do you really believe
That love is possible, I wonder can you see

I look into your eyes and visions flash
But I can't catch them cause their moving much
to fast
I reach into your heart and touch your soul
But I can't feel it cause my conscience is too old
I have a feeling that I'm, I'm losing ground
I can't believe this is all going down

My head is spinning at the speed of light
My vision's blurry but it's never felt so right
My heart's on fire and my mind is too
I can't believe that there's nothing I can do
My dear lover for the first time in my life
I'm in love and sure feels out-of-sight

I know that I can't fight this
I know I can't.
I know that I can't fight this
I know I can't

Why Don't U Know?

You think you know me
But you really can't see me at all
Your point of view's askew
Just like graffiti on the wall
U walk in two directions at the same time never
getting there and when you don't you Zen out
and claim that you don't care
Well maybe you don't or maybe you don't
realize
There's more to what's true in this life than
what seeps through your eyes
You Jack the ripper, Dr. Jekyll, Mr. Hyde
Run and hide when you rip your Jack playing
slow suicide.
How can you sleep at night or maybe that's why
you don't
Did you ever stop and think?
Or will you won't?
Why don't you know?
Why don't you know?
Why don't you know?
Why don't you know?

A Place in the Heart

Four o'clock on a working afternoon
The weekend came but it couldn't have come a
day too soon
I got up and took a look around
But I could not help feeling down
So I walked into Velvet's Bar
The only place I know where they never care
who you are
There she was sitting all alone
And I don't know why but I asked her if I could
take her home
She looked surprised but then she said alright
But please don't bother if you're not gonna stay
all night
She just smiled when I asked her for her name
Said what's the difference tomorrow it is all
gonna be the same

She said, I won't mind when you go away
But it's alright if you wanna stay
I'm not asking for a brand new start
I'm looking for a place in the heart

We drank wine and laughed all through the
night
So much to talk about we didn't even notice the
daylight
I got up and took a look around
But I could not find a single reason to be down
She kissed me soft and sighed as I held her tight
And that is the first time I can remember it
feeling right
She sipped her wine and kissed me on the
cheek
And the silence was broken when I found the
nerve to speak
I said, is it okay if I call you mine
Even if it's only for a time
I thought I was being really smart
But I never had a place in the heart

I never had a place in the heart before
I never even knew it could exIst
Now I've learned how to make a start
I finally found a place in the heart

I never had a place in the heart before
I never even knew it could exist
Now I've learned how to make a start
I finally found a place in the heart

It's Down to This

So it comes down to this?
Funny, sometimes you can't tell a hit from
a miss.
Then again, what's the difference
anyway?
It's all the same.
What you see is what you get.
But it aint always worth the price you
pay.
Who would ever guess I'd be here again?
Left out, lost from inside, bleeding open,
all that was pure.
Damn! What a waste.
The taste regurgitated thick like paste.
Stuck in my throat and I choke on my
words coming back to me.
Another first kiss which really is the last
and they never last, cause past is past
And there aint no getting back

No 'where we once belonged',
Just another sad song, sung by them who
never really knew.
So it's blew, oh pardon me, blown.
Maybe if I'd known what you thought I
didn't know.
You might not have been so quick to think
what you thought.
But I thought if I could see you, deep into
you, I'd know what's in your heart.
And if I'm something like what you
wanted, you might give me a sign.
Cause I can't read your mind
I never would even if I could cause I'm
too scared to really know.
Seems the best of me wasn't best enough
Now lust's bed sheets holds no dust, no
serenading us or kissing thus
It's all tainted rust like pliers seeping
poison in the blood of love...infected.
I'm complete.

A hole down deep
Just a bit of emptiness, like honey's bitter
sweet.
And her hands, velvet soft, slice my flesh
like razor blades.
Leaving me hollow, a shell of what I was
or thought I should have been.
And I'm thrilled at the site of the killed
I awake in pain but still remain forget
about the past
You don't even know my name.
And so the dream is over, the game is
done.
And I'm not the one
And even with you we don't equal two.
From my broken heart love escapes and
travels beyond forbidden gates.
Often spoken of, but seldom seen
Far and away, a place I can't stay.
I am comfortable though…in her

How Does it Feel?

So things changed and now I'm not
afraid
My one regret is how long I played
I never thought that you was all the
way
And now that it's done, you're just
another day
Whatever made you think that you
could turn me on?
All you ever done was hit and run
So baby here's a trick you ain't
never seen
I'm gone before you ask where I
been
How does it feel?

You think my blood is not the same
as yours
But brand new clothes only hide the
soars
I fell but I never turned you down
And all you said was not a sound
What you call love is like razor
blades
Poison in the rust as the memory
fades
Those eyes that gleamed look dark
and cold
The true face you hid from what you
stole
How does it feel?

The Festival

Who's the egg man?
John Lennon sittin' on a cornflake in
Strawberry Fields waitin for the van.
But it never come watch the piggy's run.
As they hide from the soul construction of the
God Gun.
Sound the Festival, it's the mystical with that
pure raw science reborn in metaphysical.
Smith the Grynch and Chil Akey: we raise your
thoughts above sea level,
So the wisdom that I kick constricts the devil.
Keep your eye on the whore, she got you
hostage in war.
She knows the Mother Plane is resting on the
ocean floor.
 Some say Apocalyptic, enigma sealed and
cryptic.
But see it's coded when I kick it to confuse the
wicked.

The Four and Twenty - the coming of the
ONE.
Dimensions now arriving originate beyond the
sun.
The matador will soon be killed by the bull.
The Festival's at hand -the man has got his
hands full.

Yo' it's the Grynch you motha%^$#@ time to
grieve
I can't believe you stepped in my zone.
Chil Akey, he opened up the gate and set my
path to roam…I put my hand upon the Mad
phone.
I dial you up and enter in your cerebellum
Tearin' through your lymphatic system spittin'
venom till I swell 'em
'Bout your feelings for me you, think its cause
for debate?
Nah…I just reciprocate.
And then annihilate, I never hesitate.
Before I rip your soul apart, assimilate your
mind trait.

What you gave I'm giving back and it's a fact-
to be exact
I'm the Black Horse attack.
I'm spreading justice with the balance in my
hand
A measure of wheat for a penny agony for the
other man.
Blood to violence and violence to blood's
inherited
The Beast's despairited - the feast is merited.

Dos triple zero, then we out and in again.
The balance scrolled in blood and whispered
out into the wind.
The armies ranging north and south and east
and west
As Elijah breaks the seals we usher in the final
death.
The skies are filled with Baby Planes for what
it's worth.
The devil plots and plans we detonate beneath
the Earth.

A pound of flesh is what's required for your
sin.
The bodies of the Martyrs now alive to fight
again.
I'm the egg man – I'm the walrus.
From niggaz in the grave back into Gods is
what they call us.
Keep your ear to the ground she gets what's
coming around.
And if you stand in the way she gets to take you
down.
Some say poetic "hisdom"
Some call it racial "ism"
But see my ism is protected by the God
wisdom.
The coming dawn – the great and wonderful;
The Festival
The Festival
The Festival

Sometimes

Sometimes in the middle of making
love I cry ...
And for the life of me I don't know
why.
It's not that I don't love you can't
you see?
But I can't stand this change in me.
I never dreamed that I would ever
do you harm...
Never thought I would break the
bond.
How can I ever really be to you what
you want me to be?
How can I...when I'm still learning
how to be me?

Sometimes in the middle of a dream
I fall asleep.
I pray to the void in me my heart
will keep.
It's not that I'm unhappy and we're
still free.
But I can't believe the way life is
changing me.
I never dreamed that I would ever
do you harm…
Never thought I would break the
bond.
How can I ever really be your kind
of man?
When I'm still trying to learn to be
who I am?

And if I said I'm sorry would it help
you through…
Even though I don't know why I still
do things to hurt you.

It's not that I don't want you please
believe me.
But I'm afraid of your hold on me.
I never dreamed that I would do
you harm...
Never thought I'd ever break our
bond.
But I can't be what you need me to
be...
When the only thing that I'm really
afraid of is me.

Acknowledgments

One of the single greatest truths I have come to understand in life is that behind every note-worthy accomplishment there is a cadre of people, friends and supporters, who helped to make it happen. This is certainly the truth where I am concerned. Becoming a published author has been a passion of mine for some time. To have that dream materialize, not once but twice in the same year is more than unbelievable to me.

I want to thank my beautiful, loving mother, Dyanne Cunningham, for your unyielding love and faith in me and my ability to overcome any and all obstacles in my path. You continue to be a source of spiritual water, keeping me steeped in the healing power of God. I would also like to thank my sister, Nichole Taylor for always having my back, no matter what. You are my dearest friend and truest confidant.

Thank you to Charlene Hernandez, my very special friend for proof reading, making sure all the t's were crossed and i's were dotted. You are a big part of the finished product.

Thank you to Laura from Fiverr for the outstanding cover artwork on both *Learning to be Me* and *Love and the Game*. You are a fantastic graphic artist, I am so happy I found you. Sorry for the late hours. With Kosovo being six hours ahead, you were working, many times, well past midnight.

I would like to thank my children for being a constant source of inspiration to me, for making me become a better father, man and human being. I love you all dearly. Special Thanks to my daughter, Isabella for the beautiful paintings and free-hand drawings you contributed to this book. I am so proud of you for so many reasons.

Lastly, thank you to all my friends and family for your support. And to anyone reading this, thank you for buying this book and helping me to make my dream come true. God bless you all.